True Life

Alexander Hamilton

Monika Davies

Consultants

Timothy Rasinski, Ph.D.
Kent State University

Lori Oczkus, M.A.
Literacy Consultant

Publishing Credits

Rachelle Cracchiolo, M.S.Ed., *Publisher*
Conni Medina, M.A.Ed., *Managing Editor*
Dona Herweck Rice, *Series Developer*
Emily R. Smith, M.A.Ed., *Content Director*
Seth Rogers/Noelle Cristea, M.A.Ed., *Editors*
Robin Erickson, *Senior Graphic Designer*

The TIME logo is a registered trademark of TIME Inc. Used under license.

Image Credits: Cover and p.1 Architect of the Capitol; p.5 SOTK2011/
Alamy Stock Photo; p.7 LOC [g4390.ar170100]; pp.9, 19, 20, 21, 41
Granger, NYC; p.10 World History Archive/Alamy Stock Photo; p.11
bilwissedition Ltd. & Co. KG/Alamy Stock Photo; p.13 Universal History
Archive/Getty Images; p.15 Everett Collection Historical/Alamy Stock
Photo; p.16 Stocktrek Images, Inc./Alamy Stock Photo; p.17 Museum
of the City of New York, USA/Bridgeman Images; p.22 LOC [LC-
USZ62-60769]; p.23 North Wind Picture Archives; p.25 ClassicStock /
Alamy Stock Photo; p.28 Photo Stefano Baldini/Bridgeman Images; p.30
Courtesy of the Monroe Wakeman and Holman Loan Collection of the
Pequot Library Association, on deposit in the Beinecke Rare Book and
Manuscript Library, Yale University, New Haven, CT; p.32 Glasshouse
Images/Alamy Stock Photo; p.37 Briggs Co./George Eastman House/Getty
Images; p.39 LOC [LC-USZ62-47653]; p.40 BLM Collection/Alamy Stock
Photo; p.42 Theo Wargo/Getty Images for Tony Awards Productions; back
cover United States Treasury Bureau of Engraving and Printing/
Wikimedia Commons; all other images from iStock and/or Shutterstock

Library of Congress Cataloging-in-Publication Data

Names: Davies, Monika, author.
Title: Alexander Hamilton / Monika Davies.
Description: Huntington Beach, CA : Teacher Created Materials, 2017. |
  Series: True life | Includes index.
Identifiers: LCCN 2016048650 (print) | LCCN 2016050229 (ebook) | ISBN
  9781493836338 (pbk.) | ISBN 9781480757370 (eBook)
Subjects: LCSH: Hamilton, Alexander, 1757-1804--Juvenile literature. |
  Statesmen--United States--Biography--Juvenile literature. | United
  States--History--Revolution, 1775-1783--Juvenile literature. | United
  States--Politics and government--1783-1809--Juvenile literature. |
  Miranda, Lin-Manuel, 1980- Hamilton--Juvenile literature.
Classification: LCC E302.6.H2 D34 2017 (print) | LCC E302.6.H2 (ebook) | DDC
  973.4092 [B] --dc23
LC record available at https://lccn.loc.gov/2016048650

Teacher Created Materials

5301 Oceanus Drive
Huntington Beach, CA 92649-1030
http://www.tcmpub.com

ISBN 978-1-4938-3633-8

Table of Contents

Alexander Hamilton

Alexander Hamilton's face may not be the first you'd spot in a gallery of Founding Fathers' portraits. His sensational death (a duel at dawn with pistols!) often clouds his legacy as the architect of America's financial system.

The man was a genius but also a hothead. You could count on him to go toe-to-toe with anyone who challenged him. He knew the power of the written word and used it often. He was a favorite of the ladies and a glory seeker who seemed haunted by how his legacy would be framed.

Hamilton was George Washington's right-hand man and Thomas Jefferson's most notable rival. He was also the beloved husband of Eliza Schuyler and the victim of Aaron Burr's fury.

Based on the sheer number of persuasive essays and letters he left behind, it isn't hard to imagine that Hamilton might have often asked himself, "How will history remember me?"

Hamilton: An American Musical

Hamilton's story has recently been resurrected in cultural and historical conversations. This is a direct result of the immense popularity of Lin-Manuel Miranda's *Hamilton: An American Musical*, a fun and bright hip-hop retelling of Hamilton's life. In 2016, this Broadway smash won a Grammy® Award and 11 Tony Awards®! Miranda was also the 2016 Pulitzer Prize® Winner in Drama.

From left to right: Henry Knox (seated), Thomas Jefferson, Edmund Randolph (facing away), Alexander Hamilton, and George Washington

The Hurricane

Hamilton was always a battle-ready scholar. Diving into his childhood, it is clear how he developed the **grit** and determination that would characterize his legacy.

Born **out of wedlock**, Hamilton had his trials set before he was born. His mother, Rachel Fawcett Lavine, was still married when she left her husband for James Hamilton, a Scottish immigrant.

His **rootless** father would later abandon the family when Hamilton was only 10. However, Rachel was a **resilient** woman and found ways to keep poverty at bay, such as selling groceries for income.

Sadly, the first chapters of Hamilton's life story are heavy with tragedies. Rachel died from a devastating fever that nearly took Hamilton's life as well. Left without a penny to his name, Hamilton and his brother moved in with a cousin who would later take his own life.

Facing this list of woes, an ordinary person might have waved the white flag of surrender. But it wasn't enough to stop Alexander Hamilton. This was a man who, with very little formal education, began working as a clerk. He devoured countless books, hungering for more knowledge. He had big dreams of escaping the confines of his residence in St. Croix.

Then the hurricane struck.

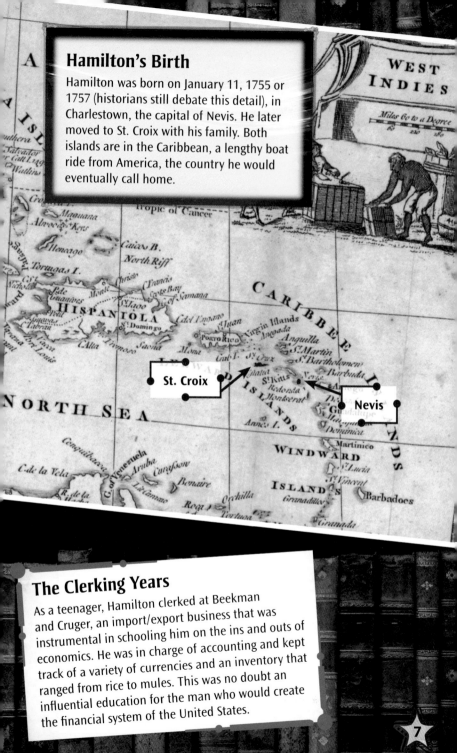

Hamilton's Birth

Hamilton was born on January 11, 1755 or 1757 (historians still debate this detail), in Charlestown, the capital of Nevis. He later moved to St. Croix with his family. Both islands are in the Caribbean, a lengthy boat ride from America, the country he would eventually call home.

WEST INDIES

Miles 60 to a Degree

St. Croix

Nevis

The Clerking Years

As a teenager, Hamilton clerked at Beekman and Cruger, an import/export business that was instrumental in schooling him on the ins and outs of economics. He was in charge of accounting and kept track of a variety of currencies and an inventory that ranged from rice to mules. This was no doubt an influential education for the man who would create the financial system of the United States.

1772

The hurricane's destructive force wreaked havoc across St. Croix. Tall trees were yanked from their roots, houses were mangled, and furniture was found strewn miles away.

Hamilton, then around 17, was horrified by the storm's impact. He wrote to his father (they had remained in touch despite his abandonment), trying to paint a portrait of the hurricane with his words: *The roaring of the sea and wind, . . . and the ear-piercing shrieks of the distressed, were sufficient to strike astonishment into Angels.*

The stirring letter was first printed anonymously in the *Royal Danish American Gazette*. Hamilton's way with words captured the attention of the public, who demanded to know the author. After word spread, a fund was put together to send the fiercely intelligent young man to America for an education.

A Rewritten Future

Hamilton ached to move beyond the **provincial** life of St. Croix. He rarely wrote or spoke of his childhood as an adult. It was complicated at best, but there's no doubt his hardships fueled his strong will and ambition.

It is incredible to consider how Hamilton rewrote his uncertain circumstances into a new future. Hamilton not only worked hard but also had the smarts to back up his work. He was en route to new opportunities—to America, the country he would help build.

A Secretive Past

Throughout his life, Hamilton was not one to trumpet about his sad past. Instead of reliving his childhood, Hamilton focused on being a forward thinker. Because of this, biographers have had to rely on extensive research to piece together the beginning of Hamilton's life.

Who Had the Letter Published?

The hurricane letter was likely shown to Hugh Knox, a minister and mentor to Hamilton. Knox probably encouraged Hamilton to have the letter published in the *Royal Danish American Gazette* (above), where Knox was occasionally an editor.

Right-Hand Man

"I wish there was a War," penned a young Hamilton. Hamilton was not afraid to fight for what he wanted. He was ready to fight for better circumstances, a free America, and his political beliefs.

George Washington recognized this trait in Hamilton, who had quickly become an asset during the American Revolution. The young man was appointed as an artillery captain and caught Washington's eye when his brigade helped the general's men retreat to safety.

Battling the British was going to require the brightest minds to devise a strategy. Hamilton was proving himself to be more than suited for the job.

A Military Family

When Washington's staff was short a member, the general knew exactly whom he wanted by his side. In 1777, Washington invited Hamilton to serve as an **aide-de-camp**. It should be noted that Hamilton's enthusiasm for his new role was limited. While he saw the potential of the opportunity, he was miles from the glory that could be found on the battlefield.

Even so, he tackled his administrative duties with vigor. Hamilton was a **shrewd** fellow. He knew Washington was the right man to have on his side. Thus officially began one of the most important political partnerships in American history.

Alexander Hamilton

1773–1776

What did Hamilton do when he first arrived in America? Before becoming Washington's right-hand man, Hamilton attended King's College (now Columbia University) in New York City. When the American Revolution hit the streets in 1775, Hamilton joined the war effort. King's College closed its doors that same year, and Hamilton never finished his degree.

Meet Aaron Burr

Remember Aaron Burr's name. Hamilton and Burr (right) would live parallel and intertwining lives. One of the many parallels is that Burr also served as one of Washington's right-hand men, but he gave up the position quickly, finding that Washington would not include him in strategic discussions.

A Founding Partnership

Imagine these two founding fathers: Washington and Hamilton. The six-foot-two Washington towered over the five-foot-seven Hamilton. Washington was a sturdy 45-year-old with broad shoulders, while Hamilton was a lean 22-year-old. Hamilton always addressed Washington as "Your Excellency."

The two men shared the same political values and ideals, but their **temperaments** were very different. Washington kept his cool and walked with a purposeful stride. Hamilton was much bolder and more passionate. He benefited from Washington's steady presence. In return, the hardworking and energetic Hamilton was the perfect secretary for the general. It almost seemed as if he could read Washington's mind. He would transform a few of the general's phrases into detailed plans or polished letters. Hamilton was the youngest member of Washington's staff but was widely acknowledged to be the general's most favored aide. It was likely a gratifying experience for the young man. He was part of an exclusive family that stood on the **cusp** of America's conflict with Great Britain.

The Little Lion

Hamilton's military family was fond of nicknames. They nicknamed him the "Little Lion."

A Critical Eye

Hamilton was by Washington's side constantly, and as such, he was more than aware of the general's flaws. His perceptive eye noted that Washington was perhaps not the strongest military leader. (He did lose most of his battles during the Revolution.) However, Hamilton never doubted that the general would be a supremely capable political leader.

A Fast-Forward

The partnership between Washington and Hamilton served both extremely well for 22 years. Here's a timeline of their working relationship from 1781 to Washington's death.

March 8, 1781

Hamilton leaves his job as Washington's secretary and returns to New York. As Ron Chernow says in his biography, *Alexander Hamilton*, "One of the most brilliant, productive partnerships of the Revolution had ended."

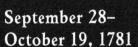

1780   1785   1790

September 28– October 19, 1781

Washington finally gives Hamilton a command during the Battle of Yorktown. The young man becomes a pivotal part of America's victory in this final battle of the Revolution, gaining the military glory he had always wanted.

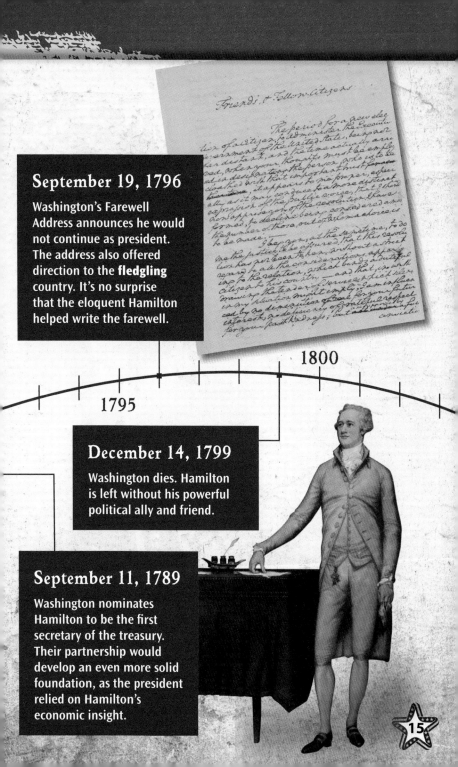

September 19, 1796

Washington's Farewell Address announces he would not continue as president. The address also offered direction to the **fledgling** country. It's no surprise that the eloquent Hamilton helped write the farewell.

1800

1795

December 14, 1799

Washington dies. Hamilton is left without his powerful political ally and friend.

September 11, 1789

Washington nominates Hamilton to be the first secretary of the treasury. Their partnership would develop an even more solid foundation, as the president relied on Hamilton's economic insight.

The Schuyler Sisters

It was probably inevitable that Hamilton would grow into a shameless flirt. His sharp mind was perfect for saying just the right thing, and his position on Washington's staff ensured that he met many fashionable women. The ladies loved him, and he likewise loved them. In matters of the heart, though, he met his match in the Schuyler sisters.

Elizabeth Schuyler

Although they had met once previously, it wasn't until 1780 that Hamilton truly took notice of Elizabeth (Eliza, or Betsey to him). Hamilton was 25 years old at the time and a **bona fide** heartbreaker. Eliza, a **fetching**, good-natured lady with direct eyes, walked straight into Hamilton's heart. In the words of another aide, he was instantly a "gone man."

On a **pragmatic** note, it wouldn't have escaped Hamilton's notice that being part of the Schuyler family would serve him well. Eliza's father was a wealthy and powerful politician in New York. Calling him father-in-law was clearly an advantage for the ambitious Hamilton.

Alexander Hamilton

Martha's Tomcat

Hamilton gained such a reputation as a flirt that some stories suggest George Washington's wife, Martha, named her tomcat after the young man.

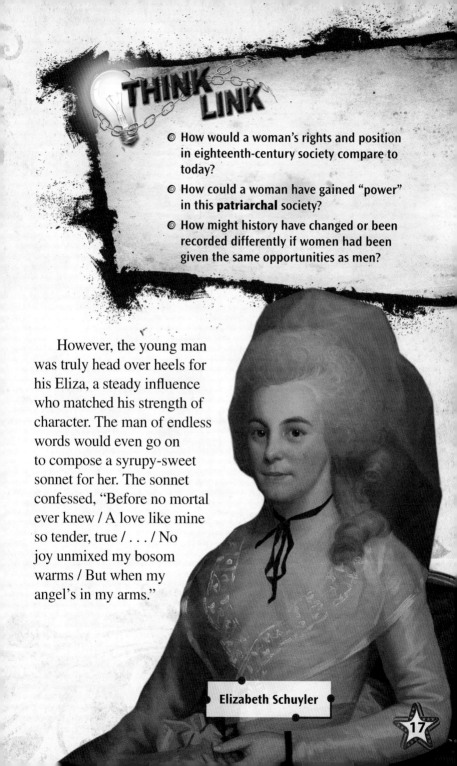

◎ How would a woman's rights and position in eighteenth-century society compare to today?

◎ How could a woman have gained "power" in this **patriarchal** society?

◎ How might history have changed or been recorded differently if women had been given the same opportunities as men?

However, the young man was truly head over heels for his Eliza, a steady influence who matched his strength of character. The man of endless words would even go on to compose a syrupy-sweet sonnet for her. The sonnet confessed, "Before no mortal ever knew / A love like mine so tender, true / . . . / No joy unmixed my bosom warms / But when my angel's in my arms."

Elizabeth Schuyler

17

Hamilton would shower Eliza with letters, using all the romantic sentiments in his **repertoire**. Eliza enjoyed Hamilton's wit, but she was most wooed by his kind nature toward her.

Their courtship was a whirlwind affair but done "properly" for its time. The two waited for her father's permission to marry. Permission was granted in April 1780. In December of the same year, they exchanged vows in the Schuyler Mansion's front parlor.

Angelica Schuyler

While Hamilton was devoted to Eliza, that didn't mean he stopped being a flirt altogether. That same winter, Hamilton met the eldest Schuyler sister, Angelica. Sophisticated, brilliant, and seductive, Angelica was always in the center of an ocean of admirers. Hamilton was entranced by her personality and ability to banter with him. They would be lively pen pals for the next 24 years, openly affectionate with their words.

This was no soap opera, though. Eliza wasn't jealous of this bond between the two people she loved most in the world. In a way, the two sisters' mutual love for Hamilton only deepened their sisterly connection. Together, the two ladies said "I do" to being Hamilton's "dear brunettes."

Two Sides, Two Women

Hamilton's attraction to both sisters gives an interesting insight into his character. Eliza and Angelica would have appealed to different sides of him. Eliza shared the same purpose as Hamilton, while Angelica had a sparkling wit that matched his own.

A Father's Permission

Eliza married Hamilton with her father's permission, which was customary for the time. Angelica (above), on the other hand, **eloped** because she feared her father wouldn't approve of her marriage to John Barker Church due to his **dubious** past.

Where It Happens

Hamilton would not sit on the sidelines while history was made. In the years following the Revolution, Hamilton worked as a lawyer, attended the 1787 Constitutional Convention, and wrote 51 essays for *The Federalist Papers*. Soon, all of his hard work would pay off.

In 1789, with some nudging from Hamilton, Washington became the nation's first president. In a wise move, he nominated Hamilton to be his secretary of the treasury. Washington also nominated Thomas Jefferson to fill the role of secretary of state.

CONTENTS.

THE

FEDERALIST:

ADDRESSED TO THE

PEOPLE OF THE STATE OF NEW-YORK.

NUMBER I.

Introduction.

AFTER an unequivocal experience of the inefficacy of the subsisting federal government, you are called upon to deliberate on a new constitution for the United States of America. The subject speaks its own importance; comprehending in its consequences, nothing less than the existence of the UNION, the safety and welfare of the parts of which it is composed, the fate of an empire, in many respects, the most interesting in the world. It has been frequently remarked, that it seems to have been reserved to the people of this country, by their conduct and example, to decide the important question, whether societies of men are really capable or not, of establishing good government from reflection and choice, or whether they are forever destined to depend, for their political constitutions, on accident and force. If there be any truth in the remark, the crisis, at which we are arrived, may with propriety be regarded as the æra in which

A   that

20

Jefferson vs. Hamilton

Hamilton had many rivals. Perhaps his most famous long-term **quarreling** partner was Jefferson.

Both men are remembered for their incredible writing skills. These skills were best displayed in Jefferson's Declaration of Independence and Hamilton's *Federalist Papers*. Hamilton was **brash**. He wasn't afraid to speak his mind. Jefferson was a quiet philosopher.

Besides their personality differences, they both had very different plans for how America should be governed. The two men were on a collision course.

The Federalist Papers

Hamilton, James Madison, and John Jay were responsible for the publication of *The Federalist Papers*, which were 85 essays compiled to encourage Americans to support the **ratification** of the Constitution. The papers live on as an interpretation of the Constitution that is still used for guidance.

Hamilton's *Report on Public Credit*

One of the most important debates Jefferson and Hamilton undertook swirled around Hamilton's *Report on Public Credit*. As secretary of the treasury, Hamilton had to figure out a way to deal with the huge **debt** left on America's doorstep following the Revolution.

Hamilton was the architect of a complex, visionary game plan for America's financial system. One of the main points had to do with the **assumption** of state debt. At the time, the nation's debt was split among the 13 states and the federal government. Hamilton openly advocated for the federal government to assume the entirety of the debt. This financial system would be the bedrock of the nation—if it passed.

Support was divided. The discussion put a spotlight on a North/South division. Most Southern states had already paid off their debts, and they were outraged that they would need to assume "Northern" debt.

Hamilton didn't have enough votes on his side. Assumption of debt was the cornerstone of his financial plan, and it was going to fail.

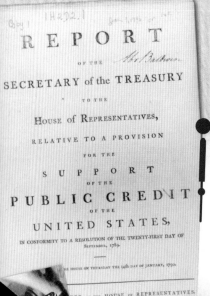

A Laborious Creation

The sole author of the *Report on Public Credit*, Hamilton combed through history and dug into multiple publications for his research. In the end, the report would total 40,000 words and include various calculations—all compiled in just over three months.

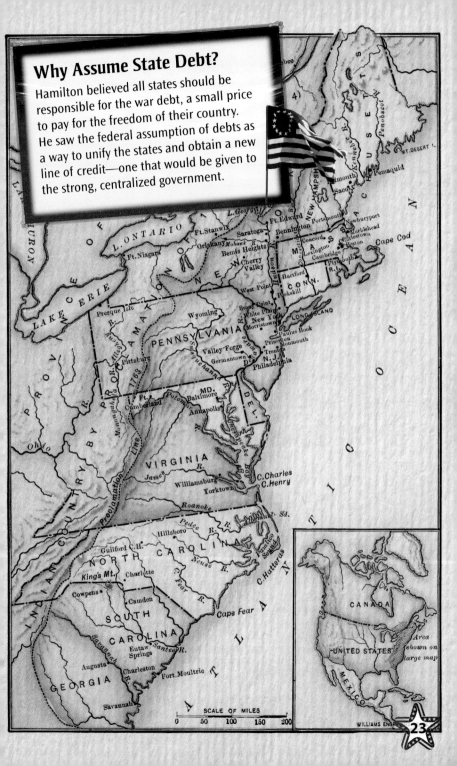

Why Assume State Debt?

Hamilton believed all states should be responsible for the war debt, a small price to pay for the freedom of their country. He saw the federal assumption of debts as a way to unify the states and obtain a new line of credit—one that would be given to the strong, centralized government.

The Dinner Table Bargain

In June 1790, Hamilton and Jefferson bumped into each other outside President Washington's home. Hamilton, usually a **dapper** dresser, looked unkempt. He was worn down from hard work. He told Jefferson if his assumption plan didn't pass, he would likely have to resign.

Jefferson pretended to be in the dark, but of course, he'd been keeping close tabs on the plan. He pledged to set up a dinner the following evening to solve the issue. The guest list would include Hamilton, Jefferson, and James Madison—the plan's fiercest **antagonist**.

Jefferson and Madison had been campaigning to relocate the nation's capital closer to the South. Hamilton, a firm New Yorker, had backed his city to be America's capital. However, Hamilton was in need of votes. A compromise was his only option.

Jefferson claimed the dinner was the backdrop for the decision that would shape America. Over the meal, it was agreed that Philadelphia would be America's temporary capital. A permanent capital would later be decided upon and named Washington, DC. In exchange, Madison promised to stop opposing Hamilton's financial plan.

Throughout their rivalry, Hamilton and Jefferson would almost always be "in the room where it happens." They were among the movers and shakers in early American history. Their ideas for government diverged greatly, and this led to legendary battles over the foundation of the nation.

STOP! THINK...

In 1940, Howard Chandler Christy painted this *Scene at the Signing of the Constitution*. Look closely and see what draws your eye.

◎ Where is the focus in this scene? What is the artist trying to highlight?

◎ What are some common characteristics of the people in this scene?

DIG DEEPER!

Difference of Opinion

The rivalry between Hamilton and Jefferson would eventually lead to the two-party system, which pitted Hamilton's Federalists against Jefferson's Democratic-Republicans. While both parties agreed on ratifying the Constitution, they had vastly different visions for the future of the United States. Let's take a closer look at some of the key aspects of each of these two parties.

Federalists

Leaders
- Alexander Hamilton
- John Adams
- John Jay

Party Supporters
- merchants
- the wealthy and educated
- popular in the coastal cities

Economic Policy
- in favor of a national bank
- supported Federal assumption of state debts
- wanted to develop credit through national debt

Foreign Policy
- opposed the French Revolution
- supported war against the French
- favored England over France

Government Views
- wanted a strong national government
- loose construction of the Constitution with implied powers
- wanted a national government that resembled a monarchy (strong ruler with advisors who were appointed and held office indefinitely)

Federalists   Democratic-Republicans

Democratic-Republicans

Leaders

- Thomas Jefferson
- James Madison
- Patrick Henry

Party Supporters

- farmers
- the "common man"
- popular in the rural South and West

Economic Policy

- against one centralized national bank
- preferred state debt vs. national debt since not all states had the same debt

Foreign Policy

- supported the French Revolution
- opposed war against the French
- favored France over England

Government Views

- wanted a strong state government
- strict construction of the Constitution with expressed powers
- wanted as little Federal power as possible
- states should reflect the citizens

The Reynolds Pamphlet

There's no denying Hamilton was an intelligent fellow. However, like any other human being, he was not immune to foolish decisions.

Hamilton could never resist playing the knight in shining armor. This trait, along with his inability to say no to a beautiful woman, would lead him into a trap—one that would lead to his fall from grace.

The First Meeting

In 1791, Maria Reynolds knocked on Hamilton's door. The 23-year-old woman was desperate and alone. Hamilton listened to Maria's tale of woe with great attention. She told him her husband, James Reynolds, had left her for another woman. She claimed to be absolutely penniless and in dire need of help. The helpless woman tugged at Hamilton's heartstrings, and he promised to open his wallet to support her.

That night, he knocked on her front door, money in hand. In return, Maria opened her door to the politician. Instead of walking away, Hamilton began a relationship that would **capsize** his legacy.

It is debatable exactly why Maria targeted Hamilton. What is certain, though, is that Hamilton's ill-advised affair turned into the perfect blackmail opportunity for her dishonest husband, James Reynolds.

Maria Reynolds

What about Eliza?

When the affair surfaced, little is known about how Eliza reacted to the humiliating scandal. While it can be assumed that she was heartbroken and devastated, Eliza forgave Hamilton. The two remained married, and Eliza continued to support her husband.

Extortion

James Reynolds began blackmailing Hamilton, giving him "permission" to continue seeing Maria as long as he paid the couple to keep his secret. He collected payments from Hamilton on a semi-regular basis. James claimed that if a payment wasn't made, he would go straight to Eliza. The affair ended in 1792, after a year of payouts.

Fraud?

In 1797, *The History of the United States for the Year 1796* was published. Two chapters explain the money paid to Reynolds to keep the affair hush-hush. However, the publication spun the blackmail differently. Since Reynolds had a criminal reputation, the association between the two men made the author conclude that Hamilton had been **embezzling** government funds. The author stated that the payouts must have been to keep Reynolds silent.

A Lengthy Headline

It is called the Reynolds Pamphlet today, but the document actually had a much lengthier headline. The entire title is *Observations on Certain Documents Contained in No. V & VI of "The History of the United States for the Year 1796," in Which the Charge of Speculation Against Alexander Hamilton, Late Secretary of the Treasury, Is Fully Refuted. Written by Himself.*

OBSERVATIONS

ON

CERTAIN DOCUMENTS

CONTAINED IN NO. V & VI OF

" THE HISTORY OF THE UNITED STATES
FOR THE YEAR 1796,"

IN WHICH THE

CHARGE OF SPECULATION

AGAINST

ALEXANDER HAMILTON,

LATE SECRETARY OF THE TREASURY,

IS FULLY REFUTED.

WRITTEN BY HIMSELF.

PHILADELPHIA:

PRINTED FOR JOHN FENNO, BY JOHN BIOREN.

1797.

Hamilton's Response

How does a man obsessed with his reputation answer this half-true slander? He publishes a long-winded "tabloid" on the scandal.

The Reynolds Pamphlet contains almost 100 pages detailing the entire affair. Every intimate detail was laid bare. Hamilton's strategy was to use his knack for words to solve the mess he was in. It worked . . . but he only thought about protecting his past achievements. The scandal shredded his reputation and his marriage. Any political aspirations that Hamilton might have had were **quashed**, and his career was undeniably sunk.

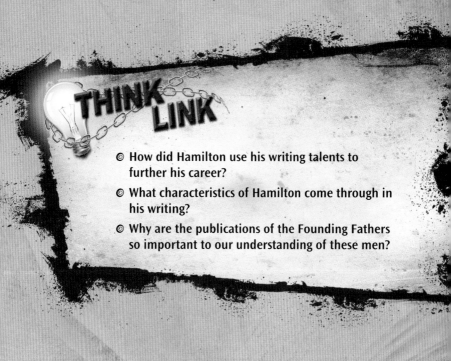

THINK LINK

- ◎ How did Hamilton use his writing talents to further his career?
- ◎ What characteristics of Hamilton come through in his writing?
- ◎ Why are the publications of the Founding Fathers so important to our understanding of these men?

Burr vs. Hamilton

There is a name that echoes in every retelling of Hamilton's story—a man whose life almost seemed to parallel Hamilton's own and who would cross paths with the political giant for decades. However, while we remember Hamilton alongside his accomplishments, his greatest foe is simply remembered for starting the duel of the century. Meet Aaron Burr, the man who helped write Alexander Hamilton's last chapter.

Aligned Beginnings

The two men could have been on the path to a great friendship. While Burr came from an **affluent** background, he was orphaned at a young age. Both men lacked the support of a family, but they fought to build lives in America.

The comparisons continue. The men were about the same height and extremely attractive to ladies of the time. Each would act as a lawyer following the American Revolution. Most importantly, both wanted to rise in the political world—which put them at odds.

Aaron Burr

Opposing Temperaments

Hamilton was a headstrong intellect, and his wit was always sharp and ready for a verbal showdown. Burr instead preferred to be a man of secrecy, listening instead of talking. He was cautious and **cryptic** when it came to his stance on various issues. This was in direct contrast to Hamilton, whose opinion was always known—and often stated in lengthy speeches or even lengthier essays.

Burr Versus Schuyler

Hamilton and Burr's political rivalry was a long time in the making. In 1791, Burr nabbed the New York Senate seat from Philip Schuyler, who had been in the seat for years. Hamilton had been counting on his father-in-law's support in the Senate, and Burr ripped away that backing.

Alexander Hamilton

Clashes

It was a struggle for Burr to watch as Hamilton gained more and more power in politics, especially since Hamilton actively knocked Burr down a few pegs.

1800

The presidential election of 1800 was full of twists and turns. Federalist John Adams received only 65 votes from the **Electoral College**. Democratic-Republicans Jefferson and Burr each received 73 votes from **electors**. Due to the tie, the decision went to the House of Representatives. The House was divided in its loyalties, but the majority seemed to side with Burr.

Thomas Jefferson

When asked his opinion, Hamilton weighed his options. While he disagreed with Jefferson on nearly every topic, Hamilton felt Burr was the more dangerous choice. Hamilton thought that Burr was **unprincipled** and solely interested in his own gains. Hamilton decided to use his favorite weapon of choice to encourage representatives to vote Jefferson into office—letters bursting with fierce statements. On February 18, 1801, Jefferson was elected the third president of the United States.

Did Hamilton influence the tiebreaker and eventually hand the presidency to Jefferson? Perhaps. Burr certainly thought so. His venom was now aimed directly at Hamilton.

1804

In 1804, Burr ran for the position of governor of New York. While Hamilton no longer had much political **clout** aside from his famous name, he fought fiercely to oppose Burr. Burr lost the election by a substantial margin. All of this added fuel to the vengeful fire growing inside Burr.

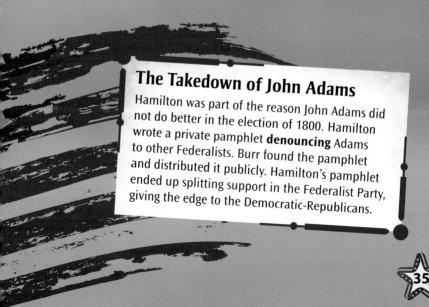

The Takedown of John Adams

Hamilton was part of the reason John Adams did not do better in the election of 1800. Hamilton wrote a private pamphlet **denouncing** Adams to other Federalists. Burr found the pamphlet and distributed it publicly. Hamilton's pamphlet ended up splitting support in the Federalist Party, giving the edge to the Democratic-Republicans.

The Challenge

It was a stray letter in a newspaper that led to history's most infamous political duel. The letter contained vague details about a dinner Hamilton attended where he denounced Burr as untrustworthy.

Burr was still recovering from his latest political defeat, and Hamilton's insult boiled his blood. Enough was enough, Burr decided—it was time for the two **adversaries** to meet on the dueling ground.

July 11, 1804

On that breezy, fateful day, Hamilton and Burr faced each other. When word was given, the two political rivals raised their arms, pistols in hand, and fired. The shots rang out, the explosive sound breaking through the calm air.

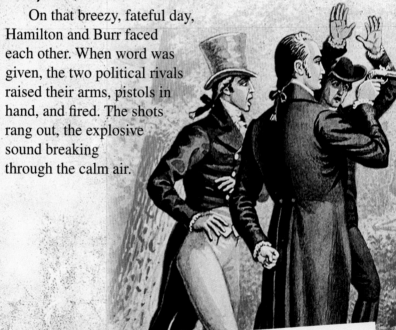

Throwing Away His Shot

There is documented evidence that Hamilton may have decided to throw away his shot before the duel even occurred. His farewell letters to his loved ones seemed to make that point clear. He also asserted multiple times on his deathbed that he never intended to hurt or kill Burr.

Burr's aim was deadly accurate, slicing through Hamilton's rib and carving up his liver. Hamilton fell to the ground in tortured agony, announcing, "I am a dead man." A day later, death claimed Hamilton.

The bullet discharged from Hamilton's pistol would later be discovered in a cedar tree, a few feet from where Burr had stood.

Regrets

There isn't a lot of evidence that shows Burr was highly **remorseful** over the duel. In fact, he would often laughingly refer to "my friend Hamilton, whom I shot."

However, Burr once revealed a sliver of regret, saying, "I should have known the world was wide enough for Hamilton and me."

Dueling Code

Dueling was considered the "gentlemanly" way to settle a disagreement. Most of the time, the challenge never actually amounted to a duel. If it did, the two men would meet before the sun was up (since duels were illegal), accompanied by their seconds (backup duelers), and a doctor (who would turn his back so he could deny witnessing the event).

After the Duel

When word spread of Hamilton's death, there was no one as devastated as his **staunchest** supporter, Eliza. She had weathered the storms of Hamilton's life with a grace that is barely documented. Through the hard times and the more devastating times (such as the death of their son), Eliza stood by his side. To his dying day, Eliza was Hamilton's greatest comfort.

It would be a mistake to characterize Eliza as simply the passive spouse of a great man. Eliza was a great woman of her own, made of stern **resolve**. She would not only become the keeper of Hamilton's legacy but also would go on to compose her own legacy separate from her late husband.

Preserving Hamilton's Legacy

It is said that "history is written by the victors," but even further, it is written by the victors who live the longest. During his life, Hamilton made many enemies who had a lot of political power. The list includes Thomas Jefferson and John Adams, who would craft their own versions of major events. They downplayed Hamilton's contributions, casting him in an unflattering light. Hamilton's legacy might have been smudged beyond recognition if it hadn't been for Eliza.

Worn Words

Eliza (below) always kept Hamilton's words close to her heart. She stored Hamilton's first sonnet to her, well worn and well loved, as well as his farewell letter to her, in a small pouch that she wore around her neck.

Missing Correspondence

It's interesting to consider how Hamilton was so intent on filling the world with his words, yet Eliza left behind very few of her own words for historians to pore over. Hardly any of Eliza's correspondence survives, and it is widely believed she burned all of her own letters.

Historians are forever indebted to Eliza, who dedicated much of the last years of her life to collecting and cataloguing pieces of Hamilton's life. She sent questionnaires to the men who had worked with Hamilton and gathered his correspondence with Washington. She had up to 30 assistants examining his papers to help her build a biography on her late husband.

The biography was her tribute to Hamilton. Sadly, the final copy wouldn't be published until seven years after her death.

Continuing On

In 1806, Eliza cofounded the New York Orphan Asylum Society, the city's first private orphanage. She spent 42 years directly involved with the orphanage and was its first directress. She expertly handled its financing in a manner that would have made Hamilton proud.

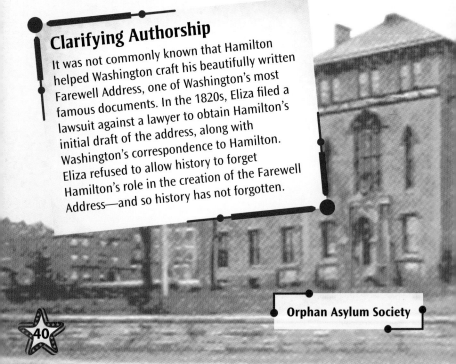

Clarifying Authorship

It was not commonly known that Hamilton helped Washington craft his beautifully written Farewell Address, one of Washington's most famous documents. In the 1820s, Eliza filed a lawsuit against a lawyer to obtain Hamilton's initial draft of the address, along with Washington's correspondence to Hamilton. Eliza refused to allow history to forget Hamilton's role in the creation of the Farewell Address—and so history has not forgotten.

Orphan Asylum Society

Her list of accomplishments doesn't end there. She also raised money to build the Washington Monument and opened the Hamilton Free School, the first school in Washington Heights in New York City.

Her Death

Eliza lived to a **stately** 97 years of age. She would go to her grave still in love with Hamilton, who likewise greeted death still devoted to his generous wife. His farewell letter to her said, "I shall cherish the sweet hope of meeting you in a better world. / Adieu best of wives and best of Women." They are buried next to each other in New York's Trinity Churchyard.

Their Children

Eliza and Hamilton had eight children in total. Their eldest, Philip, tragically died in a duel defending his father's honor prior to Hamilton's own death.

Hamilton's Story

Learning about the ups and downs of the relationships in Hamilton's personal and political life gives a well-rounded picture of the brash, relentless scholar. He was human and made mistakes just like anyone else. Despite his personal flaws, there is no denying that his accomplishments have stood the test of time. Hamilton's influence still resonates through America.

Hamilton spent his life mulling over his legacy, how to ensure that his story was shared after he was gone. Most Founding Fathers have volumes of biographies dedicated to their lives. However, Hamilton, the man perhaps most concerned with making a mark on his nation, would instead fade into the background.

That is, until now. With a successful Broadway musical about Hamilton's life, there has been renewed interest in this great man. Maybe now that his story has been told, he will begin to get the credit that he deserves.

The best way to remember Hamilton is perhaps through his own words. In the first of the many political pamphlets he wrote, Hamilton signed off in the role he most valued: "A Friend to America."

Learn More

Are you ready to dive deeper into Hamilton's life story?
Listen to the soundtrack of *Hamilton: An American Musical*,
Lin-Manuel Miranda's hip-hop version of Hamilton's
life. If you're ready for a bigger challenge, tackle Ron
Chernow's *Alexander Hamilton*, one of the best and most
comprehensive biographies written about this complex man.

Glossary

adversaries—enemies

affluent—rich; well-off

aide-de-camp—a military officer who acts as an assistant to a senior officer

antagonist—someone who opposes another person

assumption—to take on the funding of the state's debt

bona fide—genuine; real

brash—strong or harsh

capsize—overturn

clout—influence; power

cryptic—mysterious

cusp—a point of transition

dapper—neatly put together

debt—something owed

denouncing—criticizing or rejecting

dubious—untrustworthy or suspicious

Electoral College—a chosen group of people from each state who elect the president and vice president

electors—the members of the Electoral College who have the right to vote in an election

eloped—got married in secret

embezzling—stealing money from a place of employment

fetching—attractive; appealing

fledgling—inexperienced or underdeveloped

grit—courage, strong character and nerves

out of wedlock—born to parents who are not legally married to each other

patriarchal—controlled by men

pragmatic—sensible

provincial—related to an unsophisticated location

quarreling—fighting or arguing

quashed—crushed

ratification—official approval of a document

remorseful—regretful

repertoire—a set of skills that a person has

resilient—strong; tough

resolve—strong determination

rootless—having no family ties

shrewd—perceptive; clever

stately—impressive

staunchest—most consistently and firmly loyal

temperaments—people's usual attitudes or moods

unprincipled—lacking morals

Index

Check It Out!

Books

Chernow, Ron. 2004. *Alexander Hamilton*. Penguin Group.

Collins, Paul. 2013. *Duel with the Devil: The True Story of How Alexander Hamilton & Aaron Burr Teamed Up to Take on America's First Sensational Murder Mystery*. Crown Publishers.

Fritz, Jean. 2011. *Alexander Hamilton: The Outsider*. G. P. Putnam's Sons.

Miranda, Lin-Manuel, and Jeremy McCarter. 2016. *Hamilton: The Revolution*. Grand Central Publishing.

St. George, Judith. 2009. *The Duel: The Parallel Lives of Alexander Hamilton & Aaron Burr*. Penguin Group.

Videos

American Experience. *Alexander Hamilton*. PBS.

The White House. *Lin-Manuel Miranda Performs at the White House Poetry Jam*.

Websites

Atlantic Records. *Listen to the Original Broadway Cast Recording of Hamilton: An American Musical*. http://atlanticrecords.com/HamiltonMusic/.

PBS. *Code Duello: The Rules of Dueling*. http://www.pbs.org/wgbh/amex/duel/sfeature/rulesofdueling.html.

Try It!

In 2015, the hit Broadway play *Hamilton: An American Musical*, written by Lin-Manuel Miranda, was an instant success. The musical tells the story of Hamilton's life through hip-hop, song, and rhythmic storytelling. Imagine you are a musical playwright like Miranda and your job is to select another historical figure to showcase. Before putting pen to paper, you have some work to do:

- Make a list of historical people you might want to write about. They can be politicians, like Hamilton, or they could have had another profession.
- Look at your list and select a person that many people might not know about.
- Research the life of this person. Make sure you include biographical and important career events.
- List these events on a timeline, and select five major events to showcase. Remember, these events should have some significance as to why the person is historically important.
- Write a song for each of the five major events. Get creative. The songs can be any genres that you'd like.
- Give your songs to a friend for suggestions about what to add or change.
- Put the songs in order, and create a final draft of your musical play. Give it a unique and interesting title.

About the Author

Monika Davies is a Canadian writer and traveler. She loves reading about the movers and shakers of American history, especially since the Founding Fathers were some of the most brilliant thinkers who ever lived. Davies graduated from the University of British Columbia with a bachelor of fine arts in creative writing. She wrote this entire book listening to "The Room Where It Happens" from the *Hamilton* soundtrack.